THl

Sunita Thind

Wild Pressed Books

First Edition.

The publisher has no control over, and is not responsible for, any third party websites or their contents.

THE COCONUT GIRL @2020 by Sunita Thind
Original cover image by Abi Snathan
Cover design by Tracey Scott-Townsend
ISBN: 9781916377417
Contact the author via twitter: @SunitaThind

English language edition.
Published by Wild Pressed Books: 2020
Wild Pressed Books, UK Business Reg. No. 09550738
http://www.wildpressedbooks.com

This book is dedicated to my wonderful husband and love of my life Peter, and my magnificent Samoyed male Ghost.

My amazing, kind and strong mum Jesbinder, beautiful younger sister Kavita (whose name means poem in Punjabi), Dad and handsome loyal and loving brother Rishdeep, My Peji Puha (paternal aunt) six other puha and family in Malaysia, Dadima and Nanima and Nana

My luminous mother-in-law Linda Goodman-rest in peace,

My incredibly kind, charismatic father-in law who is always there for us.

My fabulous most chatty, kind hearted effervescent Grandmother-in-law Muriel Crofts and stunning and delicately kind Nanna Goodman

Also Dr Asher, Dr Jayaprakasan, the Oncology, Chemo, Fertility teams and everyone who saved and is still saving my life from Ovarian Cancer at the excellent Derby Royal Infirmary.

THE COCONUT GIRL

Contents

Good Little Punjabi Girl

Shuffling off into extinction,
she was the inferior prototype.
Guarantor of good image,
chaperoned in her own culture
regurgitating Sikh psalms.
Malnourished on tidbits of Daal and Roti,
Aloo Gobi.

Preprogrammed, serving the objectives
of her cultural, familial needs and honour.
When authorised to go out (a mandatory pilgrimage)
to the Gudawara, Punjabi School or to a relative's household;
clothed in unadorned Punjabi suits and plain chunni.
Sermonizing elders brainwash her into becoming the good
    housewife,
serving mango chutney with Menhdi fingers.

How to enter this arranged marriage?
'No alcohol, no meat consumption, no gambling,
no skimpy clothes, no clubbing or going out.
No boys! Especially no boys from other races and religions!'
       "You don't want to dishonour the family and be
       disowned, do you?"
The elders pipe superiority.
Teen   pregnancies,   mental   illness,   no   divorce   or
    homosexuality, these are stoning-inducing taboos.
They say *Cover your legs, no shaving body hair,*
do not cut your hair, no waxing your mustache or plucking your
    eyebrows!
Become a doctor, a lawyer, go to university and get a good job,
Why haven't you married yet Aiyah! You are getting too old for
    having babies.
Respect your elders, always.

Constrained by the regime's demands,

you must venerate your elders.

We 'good little Punjabi Girls' don't talk about sex, sleeping around or boyfriends (openly).

Do not become a wanton enchantress or wayward mistress,

chattering about pyramids of rose champagne or diamonds.

Psychologically groomed by the Patriarch Papa.

Violently purging the westernism.

Her jewels, cosmetics, make up, phone, laptop, shimmering western garments and books are requisitioned.

Painted as a harlot.

Cosseted, contraband confiscated.

Was she belligerent and provocative like they all said?

Polluted by her western friends,

she is famished for freedom.

Her sister is exemplary in her Asian and feminine duties,

but her spirit is dilapidated, adapted to the fundamental principles of sadness.

Punjabi School

I recall the bearded brute with the citrus-bright turban.
By day an Ice cream man, Mr C –
by night a bone-chilling Punjabi Educator.
Belching and perverted, with an ignorant kind of nature.
Knuckles wrapped across by wooden school ruler.
Back hander-stinging.
Squirming after discreet slaps.
Reciting Sikh prayers...
Keertan...
Ek om...

A line up of terrified, snotty, tear-stained brown faces.
Fat Ol' Mr C stands over them, twitching with fury.
Wields his weapon of choice, a wooden ruler or sometimes
the red plastic metre stick, for added effect.
Sagging belly, curry burps, onion breath and hairy knuckles.
The Punjabi Alphabet...
Gurmurkhi Script... Urha, Erha, Eeri, Sussa, Haha, Kukka,
    Khuka, Guga...
He sweats off his fat India Gold necklace.
The ferocious scribing,
incessant repetition in cheap notebooks with chewed-up
    biros.

Sucking in the multi-coloured ink, tongue like a rainbow,
I wanted to un-brown myself.
The compulsive pleasure of this Indian bully,
the violator, the sadist.
Chanting, reciting from the dog-eared Punjabi Language text
    book,
one kid was dribbling.
The turbaned tormentor notoriously spewed profanity
in foreign tongues at befuddled students' incorrect
    pronunciation and handwriting,
Mainly mine.

Frozen Flowers

Her pale eyes still have lightening in them,
sliced peach cheekbones;
shimmering, pleated turban atop her halo
making acquaintance with death.

Fissures of spectral light,
the primary medical team have left
this heart-breaking conundrum.
She will return to sizzle and mist.
A fairy to her fairy clan.

She wears quirky jewels on her last days.
Superstition is not around her neck.
The first light is in her voice
as I grip her weak fingers
clasping a now cold, gemstone ring.

She is with unseen people and angels
enchanting us in life and now
bewitching us in death,
Cutting trenches in this grief.

These frozen flowers are no more
ushering in the mourning.
Flower-laden form sprinkled in dust
of my childhood fairies.

Who Are You Calling a Paki?

Who are you calling a Paki?
Coloured in bigotry,
knighted in racism,
the long death of the humane.
Enraged by skin colour, are you?
Dark roars within, glancing at the wreckage of you.
Who are you calling a Paki?
Stone hurler! Supremacist! Slave trader! Colonist!
Apartheid lover!
Wannabe ethnic cleanser.
Hungry and young, the demographics of discrimination,
The discolouring of you –
freedom afforded to us.
Who are you calling a Paki?
Scrutinizing my Salwar Kameez,
Spitting on my headscarf.
You said you would teach me to burn as the heretic I was.
With your ghoulish expressions
the ornamentation of
your violent racial prejudice
who are you calling a Paki?
Balaclava thug, a coalition of skinheads and Nazi might,
Kicking a sad brown face
cowering in a cluster, dazzled by fear of
expletives; of menacing tongues,
vitriolic eyes.

My Womb Is A Park Of Carnage

Bountiful harvest of organs in the cracked sink,
bodily fluids on the floor.
Buttered by fear.
Depleting fertility, the youthful marrows
health culled. Blister burns, solidified blood.
The hospital highs, vampiric skin –
a specimen in the jar of disposable beauty.

The diagnostic conundrum, monochromatic health,
no more premenstrual beauty.
Fermenting fires,
windowless in the yawning dawn.
Cerebral cortex mush, slithering out of bed,
suckling at hospital-allocated opioid.

The toilet bowl is a glistening stone monument
bedazzled by urine.
I am obituary thin today; this makes me gasp with whizzy
    delight.
I am insidious to healthy, plush, pink people.
This maddening blizzard of depression will not shed
its snowy coat —
My womb is a park of carnage.

A Child Bride Unfurling In An Adult Galaxy

Calcified in fire is the planetary body,
neutralising the shock of this secondary death.
Ectoplasmic goop is all that remains of your motherly self
groomed grimly in childhood.
What was the age of consent in this maudlin fairy story?

A Rasputin grimace,
a child bride unfurling in an adult galaxy,
abseiling into crackling conflict.
Specialized premonitions.
What lies in your arsenal not-so-heavenly?
You have been brought on warped wings.

Is my small body required to be razzed on patriarchal meat
  hooks?
Igniting and freezing, bulb flickering above –
homeless, nameless, skinny arms,
petticoats hoiked up off
my youthful pubic bone.

Bitter is your adult saliva,
tongue circling this pre-teen mouth,
tsunami of lust in your pants.
You are not civilised in your grief, Mr.
Marrying this soiled cherub?
This virtuous body is a black hole.

Lewd little man you are.
Salacious when you jack-hammered me,
love-smitten, still tethered to my umbilical cord.
Fingernails, stubble stinging, grey hair lodged
in my nubile form.

Bronze Banshees

Bronze banshees,
a gaggle of witches
hacking and cackling
with their stimulating eyes and crepe skin.
Crow's feet wrinkles and cyanide-laced tongues,
compliant in their witchcraft.

Boiling words in their cauldron,
fish wives of South India.
Dysentery in their conversation,
back-handed compliments.
Talons of the Auntie-Ji's, Didi-Ji's,
Dadima and Nanima,
besieged in their conjuring.

Gyrating in their saris,
fizzling in lusty gems – chura and tika.
These Daica are
barbed Medusas
in Salwar Kameezs.

Scarification

Scarification threading through boulders,
scaffold in damaged flesh.
I have a conscious will to do harm.
Suckle the disfigurement,
deeply facilitated in scarification.
Are these natural tattoos expendable?
Mutilation of the self is not martyrdom.
What is the legacy of these limbs of mine?
Glassless skin – scraped and scalped;
Puckered, malformed, burning, razored and knifed.

Sparkling are the stitches and sutures,
sewn into the skin.
Reddening, raw, sliced and spliced.
What are the stem cells of salvation?
Incisions-crusted blood, bones fused.
Contaminated with rough touches.
Bodily markings,
Violent inkings.
Grovelling for innocent skin,
for untouched, pristine, uncorrupted skin.

Lace Rotting

Silver eyeballs of mirrors
temple roof studded with incandescent bodies of death
beaked sun and bloodless sky.
Opalescent eggs are offerings to deities
Skull is sun dried, a skeleton of muscle
ambitious in rotting lace.
These mangled, bright ribbons through curls of hair,
a wreath of fireflies atop a feminine head.

Platinum unleashed,
power struggled,
executed with pale wrists
creamy and unblemished,
yearning to be marked.
Handcuffed in violent rubies.

Golden and morbid,
Orion's stars slant in her hair.
Panting winds, twitching in that house of joy,
not so comatose or catatonic
In this nunnery of unswayed love.

Starved of homely sorrows
whirring in a crazed household.
In this volcanic era, she is carbon dated,
tsunamis in her cataclysmic head.
A flowered flotilla, sheltered from the ensuing fires,
horrifying treats await her as she wages spectral combat,
quaking and shape-shifting
in rotting lace.

A Unicorn's Corpse

On an astral journey, unicorn revived,
once a Pegasus, Qilini.
Three-foot glass horn
harnessed in glitter.
High gloss mane,
pearl hooves.

Slipping off its imaginary back into adulthood
liquifies the innocent to soluble spirits.
Eye-candy of the fantastical,
the feminine mythic beast.

Anatomical gems, the sin to suck a unicorn dry,
sequined blood ebbing
its grave in crestfallen snow.
Heaven is now a charnel house
corpse in a skeleton of a tree,
crystal white body now sullied
its costly appetite for innocence
to cull the deathly and baptise the pure.
Reaching the celestial steeple –
Re'em.

Gallop into the fizzing cosmos,
his fabulous realm.
Hurtling towards euthanasia,
Butchered by devilment.
The legendary steed shimmers in oblivion.
Sacred creature, or winged demon
coiling in defiled flesh.

Bubble Bath

Flirting with bubbles in a bath.
The blinding highlights of my thighs,
water envies my limbs.
I behead these domes of iridescence,
pickle my arms, and my eyes pine.
This wilting process, my pruned body
scrub-a-dub-dub away the mould and chemicals.
Lush bath bombs, body ornate in gold.
Almond-oiled charcoal-black plait
coiled and serpentine.
Gaping like an opalescent fish,
coconut oil flourishes between my legs.
Rot, loss and darkness disintegrate into bathwater,
bubbles among cinnamon mounds.
The effervescent gurgle, gaseous laugh
cackling in a cauldron of fizz.
Wash away the dirt roads
of this flower house.

Glittered In Self Hate

Troubling institution
embezzled in shimmer,
in self-hate.
Coruscating brain injury,
I ate my self –
cannibalised memories
and various bodily parts.

The slut showed the virgin praise,
Titties flapping in the wind, mama states.
I disgust her with my western disorder.
The maternal longevity of mama –
I pontificate on cowardly acts.

I the scullery maid, meticulous to dirt,
fondness for bleached surface
and various cleaning products.
I am tasteless to this brutal family law,
the ornament of being a woman.
Beauty is like dust. . . rotating away with the years
painted figurine-scandalised.

Invite the lust into this male brawl
by the boys gagging for my lady parts.
Do they know these iridescent planets?
Circumventing dark instalments,
a glimmer in the twinkle and dew morn.

I make them regret they laid eyes on me.
Hand reared, scrawny, grisly and crusted with afterbirth.
Ruby-tongued, chomping canines on sagging breasts,
excavating a winter den.

I am a powerful meat eater
Surfacing from the feast of familial cannibals.
How to accommodate this ever-burgeoning body?
In fragile realms I reel from the terror birds,
parental glory in this sunrise ceremony of the mind.

Indian Gold-Sona

Gory glitz
gold plated, malleable metal
passed on, ancestral gems and ores.
Gold markets, stalls, shops, bazaar and hawkers.
Radiating bars, and jewellery and coins.
Indian wedding gold, bridal sets, bible on bullion.
This gold survey, these spousal gifts I possess.

Dowry daughter, imported
traditionally cultured.
Sacred is the bling boa
Snaking around the neck.
Elevated to the status of the Goddess Lakshmi
gilded Amritsar Guardwara.
This World, Gold, Council infesting my living room.
The dissatisfaction of dull, yellow metal
the power house of lustrous assets.
Invested, lavishly garish, is the metallic voice
the incessant sparkle will remain undiminished.

Wintering In My Cranium

Melancholy is like blood-bursting skin.
The nastier night – starless with adolescent rain.
I am an infant in my fountain of grief,
joyless, partially albino, hibernating
sequestered from the gaudy sun and its tawdry rays.

Oh, to be chandelier, bright in bejeweled pomp,
tone deaf to colour.
This fractal pattern of glee
irresponsible in bright bliss.
The realm of life, its drab hues,
always wintering in my cranium.

When did purity morph to maturity?
Dysentery of the mind – this canyon of regret
like fiery air in lungs.
Burning up on entry fantasies.
I this doll reanimated,
always in my cranium.

Dragon Dada

So much unsaid between you and I, Papa.
The red ridges in the whites of your eyes
raging.
An inferno comes from your mouth,
tainted by the regular rages.
Did I abandon you Papa, to many a white man?
Was I not a good Punjabi daughter?
Blissful inebriation,
ignorant.
This scaled and scintillating dragon
infringement.
Gestures and codes remaining and maintained.

I am not for Indian Wedding Gold and an arranged marriage,
I would be a sour bride, Papa.
I wish not to gain a caramel spouse, fresh off the boat.
The radicalised colours of my mini skirts
I hide from you, Dragon Daddy.
I am wishing to be nun-quiet.

No red wrath smeared on my cheeks,
these sallow cinnamon cheeks, Papa.
The extremities of these traditions and customs,
these womanly chained rituals and Punjabi procedures,
unspoken sorrows of Mama.

Choice did not exist in her repertoire,
pretty eastern virgin.
Not her own property, what a peculiar idea nowadays.
As I flip a roti, then a paratha on a griddle,
I do not wish for her life.
You will not see me in red and gold finery.
Maybe pink and silver lenghai,
heavily and heavenly-embellished.
Secrets passed down in mother tongue,
my ears are discombobulated.

Petrol coloured was your anger,
burning the fat off me with your sulfur slurs.
The level of scarring,
apart from my kin.

Magic In My Head

Womanly weapons, smug beauty untangling itself.
Professional envy, rotting.
Mental-bright eyes, socket-less
commiserating in woe.
Magic in my head gushes like an incandescent
   whirlpool,
suicidal colouring on my cheeks
ripe from an adolescent accident.
Why is happiness disloyal to me?
Am I compelling in melancholy,
an unnatural phenomenon when joyous?
Why do solemn birds float above in perpetual grief?
People skirt around me,
quarrelsome and pink-lipped, mourning eyeballs.
Mamma is a tyrant,
afuneral song, serenading daily.
Beastly is the slavery of my mentality,
haunted in a crawlspace.
Misery tints my mind till no sparkle is left.
I was once a bag of fire crackers,
hissing for hours.
Now fizzled out.

Ice cream Headache

Rain eroded me
not shy to go for the tear ducts,
mucus-muscled memories in motion.
Frosty migraine, ice cream headache,
mouth swelling with lustful temper.
Iced eyeballs
lurking behind gelatinous retinas,
oyster-like tumours.
The desire to ingest sequins of jubilation
for this not-so-familial occurrence
thaw the forehead
saturate the dazzle.

Oil fields slick with scorn,
acidic-thrashing in a terror swirl.
Joints bend in an ambidextrous haze.
Freaky streaks beneath the funeral shrouds
squinting and slurring from the deadly frozen hemicrania.
Stretching, rubbing, harshly wipe me of these metastatic cells
crashing down in a quiet way
the soul-withering days.
Grappling hotly at the respiratory tract, this throat demon,
throttle me.
Skin, muscle and bone – dead-end colourings,
prized loner in the grime gaslight.

Serpentine Chuni

Vying to be seen, beneath the serpentine Chuni,
onyx tresses like octopus tentacles, oily darkness
choke-hold audiences of drunks
Her courtesan ancestors slip away in their veiled shame.
Chura tantalize her arms.
The night she came of age,
her unadorned mane became bejeweled hair
tenderized, pulsing in the Kathak dance
walking on silver – a fire!
Flashing as a cadence of harlots.
Her dancing bells tinkle, her nose ring jingles.
Solid gold and regal-heavy in gems,
chiming jewelry,
throbbing to the thunderstruck media.

Brain Fog

This grievous brain is vanishing,
wiping shadows from mirrored glass
casting a glamour over him,
eyes so glassy with internal ghosts.
Evil pacing, unruly incandescence,
companions perished.
In the ancient dark I wish to be newborn in the violence of
    love.
Rancid brain fog,
sparkling with magic ions –
fantasy thought patterns.
Stinging notions and moronic endings,
blackmailing grand gestures,
familial estrangements.
Their killing irises,
this loathing of I.
The bulk of glowing anguishes
concocts a ruse, sinister thrills.
A homage to the heartless, the loveless,
the once-motherless.
Joyriding towards lavish funerals, filthy cities;
motherly dysfunction.
The sound of my life dripping away.

Hush Tones Of Doom

Under a rust sun, muzzled,
I exhume my own dread.
Dazed constellations
hoist twilight.
The gold climes,
opulent shock.
These cascading failures,
necrosis of my optimism.
In the underworld
I grope for the bogey man,
hush tones of doom
symptomatic of this starry terror,
newborn dread in amniotic brine.
Organs devoured from the inside.

Lust-Muscles Of Forefathers

The memory of muscles,
something remains even when gone.
Shame punished them, coming of age
to touch what is living.
Bloody scratches,
unnatural stains
jewel bright, cherryade-red.
Foaming waters gave way to constellations.
Rotten seeds, graveyard flowers,
petals swarmed near coffins.
Distilled gems in sunlight waves
quivering for days.
These bloodshot roots, unruly soil of the soul
death-drenched.
Fury-imitating flames.

Auditioned for angels, the exiled ones
frothed from immortal joy.
Angel anger shimmered in my bones,
I was desecrated by the lust-muscles of my forefathers.
The icy clink of glasses, the liquor swirl
necrosis of the sane.

Fire-gored and blackened
this dull, native girl is imbibed.
The necessary evil, engine of the pedophile
contemplating lethal happiness.
In deathly mirrors, vice hits her thrice
for the muscled lust of her forefathers.

Radiation Rainbow

Correlated shimmer of radiation rainbow,
solar systems of brightness betwixt my head.
Micro planets spinning radiantly
with fanatical brilliance, in undulled irises.

Dreaming and beaming in languages of colour,
psychotropic drugs.
Vanquishing a diminished mind,
stalling in its death process,
radiation rainbow.

This angry crust
a curse over my head.
This coruscating migraine,
a planetary mass.

Tempered Stars

My mind is a charnel house,
rubble of brain, neurons misfiring
supernova brightness now ash,
the ash of synapses.
Leaden pathways
prematurely aged in the right hemisphere,
lustful compulsions,
wireless dreams
debt of night time terrors.
Red spring and blackening summer,
squid ink black is my cerebral matter.
Intellectual wilderness
neural demise
poisonous to the egocentric self.
Interior dialogues
split the head open, tempered stars spill over.
Archaic misery
betwixt boredom and terror.
The balm of booze entices the miraculous skeleton.
Interstellar journey
within morphine's reach.
How to devastate a diamond
dulling its coruscating sheen?
Pained I am, by its shimmering ebullience –
this phantom pain, fused and unexplainable.

The Lucidity Of My Brain

The lucidity of my brain permeates animate and inanimate
   memories.
Cold solders my sparkling eyeballs
mirror-balled, disco-brightened.
This sickening disquiet
festively dressed in a hindrance of Christmas pleasantries.
I was slayed like a demon with ribbon-coloured blood.
Embroidered under twilight beams, I yearned for punishment,
slack, then quivering from a profusion of soft smacks.

I remember her,
She had skin with the luster of mother-of-pearl.
Now she convalesces like a sunken ship,
shimmering in the rain.
She is not a tamer of the light,
she never lets me deviate from discipline,
detesting my unruly manner.
Dainty, pallid lady with blue-veined skin.
I wore a silver frock with gold tulle.
She was astounded by my errors in childhood.
She said I had mermaid hair, and butter song in my voice.
Her monstrosity jinxed me,
Like a black dragon spewing green mercury,
Blowing poison in my face.

Siren Song

Grief-stricken siren with mermaid hair
sings of far galaxies and watery planets.
Serenades with bewitching notes,
glitter-scaled fish tail.
Earth quaking water,
beyond the grime and sea slime
marine creatures.
Who is the mermaid wrangler?

On ill tides, blackening her ballad
not so melodious, beguiling others.
Prismatic irises boil with her siren song.
Light refracts through her deranged soul
enticing seafarers to watery suicide
with her rainbow lullaby.
Awaiting them in underwater canyons,
lacing men with their lusty laments.

Nestled between ocean butterflies,
ash-silver plaits spiral in half-frozen ocean.
Her victims are blinded
by her venomous pheromones.
She delivers a corrosive lullaby
painting death on the lips of her sailors –
barnacle-clustered, sea-mildewed.

False Gods and the Faithless

Stunted by deformity of faith,
force-fed scripture like a corn-fed duck
I grieve for my own faith.
Religious contraptions and false gods
hampered by dogma,
icons of irrelevance.
I was a thorny schoolgirl
of toffee-hued skin
listening to spiky sermons,
gagged at the Gurdwara.
The once heady bustle of my head is now dutiful,
a funeral of flowers in my hair
in an almost-Alzheimer haze,
an afterlife in this waking hell.
Conditioned to submit to some Guru,
muck-minded
in fascination of western wickedness –
all this debauchery between my thighs
(spouts an oh so pious priest).

Falsified in Indian silks,
the scornful mama adorns me with Indian gold.
Veiled with a chuni in Prarathana Hall.
Ruffling at brain dreams in the Langar Hall,
slopping aloo gobi.
Selectively amnesiac of my mother tongue
disemboweled of free will,
a discontented, phosphorous bird
With wings of glimmer

Reincarnation Queendom

Sister, do you await me in the next life,
in your celestial queendom with your upgraded software?
I am buffering, erased by death,
reincarnated in Aurora Borealis
circumventing hell and the Grim Reaper,
the city boils over.

A blazing trail like scarlet macaws –
alighting – screeching as if their feathers were immolated,
no power of flight
to develop their astral muscles.
Fresh casualties gagging for souls,
castle in the clouds.

Will surrogate angels fire brimstone on me?
Eating witches' flowers
on this theatrical jaunt through life.
My feuding genealogy,
controversially tangled.
In the flaming atmosphere, I hawk my karma –
this fashioning newness of cells.

Virgin Brain

Filtered pure with astonished kisses
slaughtered in bliss, this petty trance.
A holocaust of desire, unbidden
incites a ferocious tang of sleaze –
she ravenously rewrites her virginity.

In her loch of starlight and fireflies
lustful vapours undulate in her body.
Golden screech and screw in the
dolls-house seance of her brain.
Salty gales of panting,
spectral fires and filth in her virgin brain.

Sexy, sad and jittery like an explosive geode
she cauterizes her love with winking kisses,
ode to her newbie fertility.
No eggs rotting or putrefying with age
within womb walls

Denouncing the saga and flame of sex
she is hotly stolen.
Divinely ripe she is,
the ferocity of this tongue lust.
Swooping in on the undistracted mystique
Of her between-the-legs-purity.

Baby Doll And The Adult Apocalypse

The obscene scents of summer childhood,
why corrected in adulthood?
To run and play
daintily flailing this baby doll,
snatching her delectable toys,
her clinging teddies.
Bollywood-bronzed, beehived,
starlet lying in make up
cavorts around in a gemstone sari top,
atop a mountain of ice.
Romance-kiss the boys and girls,
flamboyant lollypop colour.
Fearless thrashing in child's play
squirting water pistols.

Barbie doll with the raunchy He-man,
unplaiting My Little ponies' manes.
The sky spreads its thighs of royal blue.
Tainted Transformers, little boys up-skirting little girls
where fingers dare tread.
Drowsy from sugar-rushed candyfloss,
splintered, scraped knees.
Scratching ball-bearings on brick walls,
absorbing this make believe.
Awkward and anarchic,
rehearsing fairy tales.
Was this childhood ethically sourced?
Ungovernable lights of sibling rivalry
jealous of sticky fingertips.

The child was told she was the epitome of human beauty.
She hadn't known this concept before the gilded mirror
    cracked
on her thirteenth birthday.
When the adult apocalypse began.

The Interlude Of This Feminine Plague

I was faulted, or was I a faulty specimen?
Half womanly, pillaged of an unused left ovary.
Evicted from muliebrity,
Cancer has a home in me.
Browbeaten into preventative hysterectomy,
crystallized blisters
incandescent cult in my body.
Swiveling days, recycling despair.
Crystal-teared, artistic nightmare
in my worst kind of nursery.
Plush caramel is my flesh,
thawing regret.
Esophagus unpleasantly zesty and tangy
from regurgitated digestive juices.
Biopsy – *nine centimetres* of satanic smut.
Effusion of metastatic fluids
pummel me to a bloody pulp
a splattering of feminine slop.
This installation disease, the volcano in the skin sack
cringing out chemical odours.
Childhood fragrances are scorched away
the baddies in the blood
not fortuitous against pathogen.
My biological space is now a not-so-platonic plague.
Kinky are these cancerous cells,
titillated by mutation
showered in the docility of hospital drugs.
I, ungraceful in my hospital gown, knickers banished,
flapping buttocks on display.
The sparkling hurricane of brilliant fear within,
the skirmish of a grating roar.
Feeling the loss contract –
the interlude of this plague.

The Same Freedoms As a 'Gori'

Down the chippy with Sapphire, her boyfriend tongues her
with her glitz mini skirt hoiked up.
With regularity come the profane words:
"Paki."
"Shit Face."
"Terrorist."
"Rag head."
"Go home Paki Pussy."
"Let me fuck you, Little Slave Gurl."

I'm sheltered, not allowed to shave my legs, wax my pubes,
flash my brown boobs, have a boyfriend.
Go out alone? No way!
Wear make-up, slut paint as mum calls it
or cut my knee length, blackish hair.
Smothered by parental, jellied bovine eyes.
The secret hair uncut, bushy eyebrows,
furry upper lip, yeti-like legs.
Curry fingers, onion eyes, eating with our hands like savages.
No white boys allowed.
Segregated from the 'blood foreigners with no culture'.
The fire tongue and bloodshot eyes of my 'Dada'.

I shave fuzzy legs with Daddy's razor.
Tweeze my brows into a sultry arch.
A slick of Rimmel Heather Shimmer Lipstick and Desert Rose
   Mac Blusher.
Victoria's Secret new panties and bra,
that little sequin dress from Miss Selfridge.
I think I will go commando tonight before I let Brian fuck me,
His little brown slave girl.

Slapped For Wearing Slut Paint

Referred to as a slapper,
this caramel canvas was blankly humble in form.
Ingrained Westernism on my face;
War Paint, Face Paint, Slut Paint,
brush strokes of Mac.
A symphony of antidepressants exits the body.
I stipple my face with foundation, a gore-fest of glitter.
Contouring, face-baking,
slapping mechanisms to revive the face.
Garnet red blush.
False-faced, whore.
Jeweled bindis, sequined henna, gold tattoos.
Eyelash extensions (lip fillers are maybe too far)
face jewels.
Dripping with eye sparkle pigments,
berry-black lippy stuffed down the bralette.
The metallic blue liner is binned.
"A good Punjabi daughter doesn't wear slut paint,
it's a lie on your face."
Virgin pale, clean and unblemished is the way forward, my
brown mama says.
Nanima points at the "grotesque glitter eyeshadow,"
sparkly pigment pots are smashed,
rose-coloured blushers explode
into a powder storm.
Candy floss lip gloss streaks my shameful face,
Lip lacquer soils my mouth,
Smeared off the pout before home time.

Pronounced a whorish child,
Mama was my Eastern Gestapo captain.
Tempers detonated.
On ceremonial occasions I was allowed to adorn my eyes
with Kajal
and wear a jewel bindi,

and tikka,
Raajakumaaree for the day.

Once I had secured an arranged marriage,
I would be able to adorn my face in carmine-red
Lancome lipstick to compliment my ochre complexion.
Betrothed to the Punjab.
Marriage to a 'Sidhi Sada' Apna,
from an honourable and prosperous family.

The slaps ricochet off me, familial and spousal alike.
Smarting, this dead-weight daughter in law.
Had my face been scandalized by unchaste friends?   my
    mother asked,
their loose 'white girl' morals, misfortune and lack of culture.
I had the glow of familial murder in my eyes.
No more clandestine tryst and pleasurable copulating,
or see-through tops
or cheap vodka, blue eyeliner, razzle-dazzle mini dresses.
No fumbles with Danny,
the good looking 'gora' in my class,
with the lustrous gray eyes and dirty blonde hair.
If I had got pregnant, it would have been aborted from my teen
    body straight away,
the dishonour too much.
Disowned, this 'slut' would be,
packed off to some backwater in India or Malaysia.
Emotional stoning for this mucky girl.

Truanting, secret smoking, masturbating with profanity.
Dad's backbone dipped in booze.
My mother's divine, vintage face flashes with fury.
She dips into her lace venom handbag,
entourage of cracked bodies follow her
like stardust in orbit.
They denounce my whisperings, choreograph their hate,
Punjabi propaganda.

The Coconut Girl

Brown on the outside,
White on the inside.

Sarsee Akal!
said the Coconut Girl.
Jeweled doll in a salwar kameez,
gemstone bindiya targeted on the forehead.

Kiddha!
said the Coconut Girl.
All cinnamon legs
in a profusion of glittered miniskirts.
Gin chaser, Whiskey Sour, chippy butty.
Fondled by the 'Gaura' boyfriend.

Meera Tika,
said the Coconut Girl.
Spangled headscarf gagging her.
"You are so dark, lah,"
"You must lose weight, lah,"
"Tusee Karli,"
"Tu see Muthi,"
"Did you see her niece? She got into Medicine,"
chirps from the banshees...
The aunti jee, the mummy jee...
Dadima, Nanima...

Meera Naam...
said the Coconut Girl.
Bejeweled Lengai, crystallized,
hot pink and burnt gold.
Diamonds in her hair.
The perfect bride.

Nahin! Nahin!
Said the Coconut Girl.

Mac cosmetic facade,
rhinestone-embellished hot-pants,
Holographic, stiletto boots. . .
Whiskey breath.
Her dad saw her with that white guy.

Mute was the Coconut Girl.
Manacled to her Chura.
Terraformed to her Tika.
Feasting on a banquet of curries.
A Punjabi paradox was the Coconut Girl.

My Nanima and Superstition

Nanima said not to wash my hair on Tuesdays or Thursdays.
It would bring bad luck for your brother
on one day and your sister another,
even if it was a greasy, slick, dandruff-infested, coiled mess.
Dadima would tell me to always wear black thread
or dot an onyx black spot behind my ear
to ward off the evil eye.
What is the pathology of these beliefs?
Throw chaal over your shoulder for good luck and prosperity
as an Indian bride leaves the house.
Put thai on your door to welcome new brides
in their heavy gold and garnet saris.
Take Ujwain to help cure ailments like stomach disorders –
    my aunt said it was used in Aryurveda.
Aromatic, bitter and pungent, a sweetened concoction in a jar,
shovelled down my throat, making me feel more nauseous.

Deflowering in a Flowering Inferno

A ghost poised on her lips,
longing to remain with purity.
Deflowered in a flowering inferno.
Fractions of incorruptibility,
lack of guile,
cherry tart pillow-lips
the detriment of her jailbait thigh gap.
Eye candy, looked like a trophy.
Wet dress, he was titillated.
He wanted her nubile and nude.
Pink frock, vampire feasted on her.
The unconscious movement of her tongue,

Jungli - Chudail - Kamli

"You are not *Pagli*, you are just seeking attention,"
Mum said.
I am brown girl depressed, anxious,
scratching at palms of imprinted orange mendhi.
Worn out, beaten. Mum said, "Ghisi pitee."
Treated like a leper, told not to tell anyone,
it would be disgraceful.
No more pretty window dreams,
pissing on the family reputation.
The colourism, the sexism.
Crawling into a fetal position,
the mind baffled and unemployed of joy or hope.
There are no direct sensations in dreams,
the howling mobs of familial dysfunction.
Eyeball the dark-haired vixen, wanton Jezebel,
neuro responses empty.
I was a crazy girl, 'Kamli',
Over-medicalising problems.
Guzzling and crying,
stagnating in front of the NHS psychotherapist
(The waiting list was six months).
I was told I had complex needs, no early intervention.
Map me, upload me onto a fresh slate.
De-stigmatize my miserable metabolism,
this old anatomy, brain zap, plasma broth.
Looks of revulsion at the Gurdwara and at Asian family
    weddings,
not the mother of my own desires.
Monsters codified in myths and legends,
the stage fright of life.
My psychotic departure at the Gurdwara,
chewing on the chuni,
drinking cardamon tea and overeating aloo gobi:
prescription pad fodder, a 'bhoot'.

Raksha Bandhan-Rakhri

Coloured thread around barbed wire,
gilded and jeweled on dark chestnut wrists.
Melodramatic faces on this gaggle of South Asians.
Exultation of neon dolls,
salwar kameez assembly of witch-faces,
the siblinghood, brotherhood, sisterhood.
Eulogizing the loss of Punjabi culture are the grandmothers
    of the motherland,
the toffee-toned sisters,
wearing jeweled tikkas and spangled saris.
Pestering/taunting their brothers for money,
these undaunted trophies.
Paying the toll for sibling adoration,
the pharmacy of coins.
The puha's tut at the brothers to give more cash.
Dadima and Nanima walk towards the brothers with
    methodical terror.
Their coffee-coloured skin is mosquito bitten,
her homeland is on her face.
Rakhri is observed on the same day as the lunar month of
    Sravana,
celebrating the relationships
and bonds between brother and sister.
The caramelised sisterhood serenade their brothers with
    Indian folk song,
consume celebratory sweets – *ladoo, jalebi, barifi, gulab jam*;
an annual rite on the Indian subcontinent.
Tying the talisman 'Rakhi' on the wrist of Rishdeep – this
    symbolic protection
Investing brothers with a share of responsibility.
'Raksha Bandhan' in Sanskrit: band of protection,
obligation and care.

45

About the author

SUNITA THIND is a Bedford born and Derby based female, Asian/British poet and writer. Her debut collection of multicultural poetry, *The Barging Buddhi and Other Poems*, (Black Pear Press, 2020) focused on living between two cultures, British and Punjabi. Sunita is a workshop facilitator, speaker and performance poet. She has had poetry and short stories published in various literary magazines, ezines and journals.

She has dabbled in many things including being a model, primary and secondary school teacher and trained as a make up artist. Being an Ovarian Cancer survivor she is grateful to have survived it but is not in remission yet, she is a campaigner and fundraiser for related charities.

She also loves to sing and take singing lessons and is married and has a beautiful, male platinum white Samoyed called Ghost.